Jeannette Rankin:

America's First Congresswoman

Peter Aronson

Copyright © 2019 Peter Aronson

BOOKS FOR MIDDLE-GRADE READERS

The Groundbreaker Series: Biographies about extraordinary people doing extraordinary things. This is #2 in the series. The #1 book in the series, *Bronislaw Huberman: From Child Prodigy to Hero, the Violinist who Saved Jewish Musicians from the Holocaust,* is available through Amazon.com or IngramSpark. For more info about Peter Aronson's books, including ones coming in the future, please visit the author's website at www.peteraronsonbooks.com.

Double M Books Inc., New York

Double M Books Inc.
New York

The Groundbreakers Series is a registered trademark of Double M Books Inc.

Website: www.peteraronsonbooks.com
Email: peter@peteraronsonbooks.com

Library of Congress Cataloging-in-Publication Data

ISBN 978-1-7320775-4-6 (ebook version)
ISBN 978-1-7320775-5-3 (print version)

Front and back cover designs by Ashley Byland of Redbird Designs

Layout and formatting by Polgarus Studio

Printed in the United States of America

This book is dedicated to my wonderful daughters, Mabel and Maisy, who inspire me every day and who, taking the lead from Jeannette Rankin, should strive to accomplish whatever inspires them.

(National Photo Company Collection,
Library of Congress, via Wikimedia Commons)

Contents

Introduction to Jeannette Rankin

Jeannette Rankin re-entered public life in her 80s to protest America's involvement in the Vietnam War. (Jeannette Rankin Exhibit at Georgia World Congress Center, via AVOC)

One day in May 1967, in Atlanta, Georgia, about 20 people gathered at a home to hear an elderly, yet very active, woman speak. The woman was Jeannette Rankin, 86 years old, someone they had heard of from years past. She was there to speak about the horrors of war – at a time when the United States was involved in the Vietnam War and thousands of U.S. soldiers were dying.

Rankin told the group that if thousands of women were prepared to march on the U.S. Capitol in memory of those fallen soldiers, that the war could be stopped.

Her words and actions made national news. A little more than six months later, on a wintry day, Rankin led the Jeannette Rankin Brigade on an anti-war march in Washington, D.C. Approximately 5,000 women marched on the U.S. Capitol to tell senators and members of Congress that America should stop fighting in Vietnam.

Jeannette Rankin, center wearing glasses, leading the Jeannette Rankin Brigade in a protest march against the Vietnam War in Washington, D.C., in January 1968. (Bettmann, Getty Images)

There was a good reason thousands of women were following Jeannette Rankin on the cold, snowy streets of Washington, D.C., on a march that made national news.

Although not a household name now or then, Jeannette

Rankin was one of the most accomplished women in U.S. history in the 20ᵗʰ century. She was a hero to many, loved and honored. To others, she was controversial, even a traitor to some.

Jeannette Rankin was the first woman elected to Congress, in 1916. But Jeannette Rankin was far more than the first U.S. congresswoman. A suffrage leader, a feminist, a pacifist until the day she died, some might say she was a woman 100 years ahead of her time. She stood up for what she believed in. She never backed down.

Chapter 1: Born and Raised on Montana's Pioneer Land

Jeannette Rankin was born on a ranch in Montana similar to this one.
(William Henry Jackson, U.S. National Archives, via Wikimedia Commons)

On June 11, 1880, Jeannette Rankin was born on the Rankin family ranch in beautiful Big Sky country, near Missoula, Montana, in America's still Wild West.

She was the first child of Olive and John Rankin.

At the time, Montana was a rugged pioneer's land, with settlers scattered in its wide valleys and plains, the snow-capped Bitterroot Mountains off in the distance. Montana was not yet a state, and it was only a few years after wars with the Native Americans had ended. Just four years earlier, Lieutenant Colonel George Custer and his men were killed at the Battle of Little Bighorn, across the state of Montana from where Jeannette was born.

The site of the Battle of Little Bighorn in Montana, where Lt. Col. George Armstrong Custer made his famous last stand in 1876. Jeannette Rankin was born across the state four years later. (Wikimedia Commons)

The pioneering spirit was in Jeannette's blood from the start. Jeannette's great uncle Bill had taken part in the California gold rush of 1849 and later became one of the earliest settlers in Missoula. His talk of opportunity lured his niece Olive Pickering out west. Olive was born in New Hampshire, but didn't see much of a life for herself in her home state. In 1878, she traveled west with Uncle Bill by train and stage coach and settled in Missoula. She would become one of the city's first school teachers.

John Rankin, in a later photo, came to the United States from Canada searching for gold. (Montana Historical Society Research Center)

John Rankin, like many Montana men of that era, was an adventure seeker. He was born in Canada in 1841. As a young man, he set out with his brother looking for gold in the Rocky Mountains. He didn't find gold, but he eventually settled in Missoula. John and Olive met and then married in 1879. They would have seven children.

The childhood years

Jeannette's parents provided a happy and stable home life for her in rugged 1880s Montana. As a child, she played in the fields, rode horses and helped out on the ranch. Jeannette recalled seeing Native Americans come and go past her house and attended Native American ceremonies with her siblings. As her father's ranch and lumber business grew, the family became wealthy in their small, growing town of Missoula. Because young Jeannette was the oldest child, her parents expected a lot of her.

Jeannette learned to sew and cook like other young girls, but by age 10, she already was exhibiting unusual independence and confidence, traits that would serve her well later in life. She helped her mom take care of her five younger sisters and one brother and often did a lot more than that. One day, upon seeing a horse with a wounded shoulder, Jeannette stitched her up with needle and thread. Another time, she made a little leather booty for an injured dog's leg. She was a tough, resourceful girl, growing up in a land of pioneers.

In this Rankin family photo, Jeannette is next to her mother. She took on a lot of responsibility as a child helping her parents around the house. (Montana Historical Society Research Center)

Jeannette was not afraid to speak her mind. She would debate politics and social issues with family at the dinner table. She told her father that their ranch hands should be paid a higher wage.

"She was going to be out there fighting," her brother, Wellington, recalled years later. "… She was a rebel, more or less, always."

Jeannette, lower left, with friends or schoolmates, circa early 1890s. She helped care for her siblings at a young age. (Montana Historical Society Research Center)

She learned about pacifism at a young age, something that would stay with her for her entire life. Before Jeannette was born, the white man had fought the so-called Indian Wars with the Native Americans. John Rankin would speak about the injustices Native Americans suffered at the hands of the government and settlers. John Rankin did not believe in violence, and he did not allow guns on his ranch. This attitude would have a strong influence on his daughter.

Native Americans near Missoula, Montana, circa 1890. (Archives and Special Collections, Mansfield Library, University of Montana)

By the age of 18, Jeannette began to shift away from a traditional path for girls in that era. Most girls stayed home, married and raised a family.

Not Jeannette Rankin.

Chapter 2: Young Jeannette Rankin Tries to Find Her Way

The old Montana State University campus in Missoula, circa 1900. Jeannette Rankin enrolled in 1898. (University of Montana Historical Archives, via Wikimedia Commons)

In 1898, after graduating high school at the age of 18, Jeannette followed an uncommon path for girls of that time. She enrolled in college, entering the first class of students at Montana State University in Missoula. She studied biology. But she didn't like college, and after graduating, she was uncertain about what to do next.

*Jeannette Rankin studying in the lab at college.
(Montana Historical Society Research Center)*

She lived at home and helped with the household tasks. When her father died in 1904, Jeannette, as the oldest child, took on even more family responsibility, helping run the family's affairs by handling much of the shopping, the finances and caring for her siblings.

She also had a few early jobs: as a school teacher in a one-room school house and as a seamstress at a local department store. Through a correspondence course, she learned furniture design.

But none of these things would hook Jeannette Rankin. She had yet to find her calling in life. That would slowly begin to change as she neared her 25th birthday.

Jeannette with her family, seated in the back, left, took on even greater family responsibility after graduating from college and after her father died. (Montana Historical Society Research Center)

Chapter 3: Finding a Passion that Moves Her

In 1905, Jeannette's brother, Wellington, was a law student at Harvard University in Boston. When he got sick, Jeannette traveled east to help take care of him. He recovered, and he began showing Jeannette around. They toured Boston and then traveled to New York City. For the first time, removed from the beauty and wide open land of Montana, Jeannette experienced crowded urban slums. Jeannette walked the streets of Boston and the Lower East Side, in New York City. She saw poor, struggling immigrants, crammed together in crowded, dirty tenements.

Jeannette Rankin visited this area, the Lower East Side of New York City, a melting pot of poor immigrants from Europe. (Detroit Publishing Company, Library of Congress, via Wikimedia Commons)

Seeing this human suffering opened Jeannette's eyes. It would have a tremendous impact on her.

In winter 1908, Jeannette went to San Francisco to visit an uncle. This was not long after a devastating earthquake and fire had destroyed much of the city, killing approximately 3,000 people and leaving thousands homeless. Again, Jeannette witnessed poor, struggling immigrants. She decided to help. She went to work for a settlement house, helping care for and teaching English to immigrant children.

San Francisco in ruins after the earthquake and fire of 1906. Rankin visited the city in 1908 and worked to help poor immigrants. (The H.C. White Company, via Wikimedia Commons)

Perhaps most importantly for her future, Jeannette began attending public meetings, where she learned about adult and child labor laws. She began realizing that factory working conditions and low salaries were unfair and that women and child workers were being taken advantage of.

The new field of social work caught Jeannette's attention, because she realized it would allow her to help these poor people.

In the fall of 1908, Jeannette, now 28, made an important

decision. She moved to New York City and enrolled in the New York School of Philanthropy, which later would become Columbia University's School of Social Work. She thought that by studying social work she would learn how to help poor people.

Jeannette Rankin heard Booker T. Washington, the leading black leader in America, speak about civil rights while she was studying social work in New York City. (Wikimedia Commons)

Jeannette became immersed in New York City's urban life. While in school in New York, she heard famous people, such as Booker T. Washington, the great black rights activist, and Louis Brandeis, a lawyer and future Supreme Court justice, speak about workers' and civil rights. She learned about laws that affected poor people. She worked on the Lower East Side, in the Bowery, perhaps the most notorious slum in America, filled with immigrants from Italy, Germany, Russia and elsewhere in Europe.

She wrote a sad letter to her mother describing how a mother had to put one of her three kids up for adoption because she no longer could care for him.

"I took the dearest… sweetest little boy to an orphan society," Jeannette wrote. "He was three years old and the mother had two younger ones. The father was missing. If I had been near home, I'm sure I would have wanted to keep him. He was so full of joy and life."

Rankin learned about the hardships immigrant children faced by working on the streets of New York City's Lower East Side. (Wikimedia Commons)

This opened Jeannette's eyes. She realized she needed to get involved.

Helping people as a social worker

In her late 20s, Jeannette was still a single woman. This was uncommon for those times. Most women married soon after leaving school, had children and stayed at home and raised a family, while the husband worked. But Jeannette would never marry. Reportedly, she had offers of marriage and turned them down. She made many friends, male and female, but kept her private life private. Her career - not a family – would be her life's passion and work.

Jeannette with a friend or family member, on her family ranch in Missoula, Montana. After college, Jeannette was still trying to find her calling in life. (Montana Historical Society Research Center)

By 1909, Jeannette, with her degree in social work, moved to Washington state and began working as a social worker. She helped orphaned and sick children, taking care of them and trying to find them a new home.

"I will never forget it," Jeannette said many years later. "There were too many children; only a few could be placed. Half of them returned when people changed their minds. They had suffered so much from poverty, were in such ill health, and had such bad habits, that nobody wanted them. They came back and wept in my office. All those awfully sad things about those children – I couldn't take it."

As a social worker, Jeannette soon became frustrated, because she was limited to helping only individuals one by one. She was unable to attack the root cause of the problem. So, to learn how to do this, she enrolled in the University of Washington to study finance, public speaking and government.

It was at this time that Jeannette Rankin, combining her studies with her practical experience, began realizing how she could help people on a much larger scale.

Supporters of Washington state suffrage. Jeannette Rankin, not pictured, joined this movement. (University of Washington Libraries, Special Collections, Asahel Curtis, photographer, A. Curtis 19943)

While in school in Seattle in 1910, Jeannette saw an ad in the school newspaper seeking volunteers to promote the women's right to vote – known as women's suffrage. At the time, women were able to vote only in four states - Wyoming, Colorado, Utah and Idaho. Women did not have the right to vote in federal elections, which meant they could not vote for president.

The right for women to vote was the issue that Jeannette Rankin had been looking for. This was the first issue that stopped her in her tracks – an issue that Jeannette realized needed her attention. This would change her life forever.

Chapter 4: Jeannette Rankin and Women's Suffrage

Jeannette Rankin, now 30, was about to find her place in the world. She began hanging posters in the Seattle area, urging men to grant women the right to vote in the state of Washington. Her energy and intelligence impressed suffrage leaders. Soon, Rankin was traveling the state, giving speeches in small towns and cities, at schools, lumber mills and public meetings.

"An audience of 300 people stood for half an hour listening to a little woman with a sweet voice and appealing gestures," a local newspaper reported. "The lady carefully explained that this amendment" would give women in Washington the right to vote.

The suffrage movement won, making Washington the fifth state to grant women the right to vote. Rankin was just one of the many suffrage workers in Washington, but she had found a cause that would make her famous.

Women, who just won the right to vote in the state of Washington, going to the polls in Seattle to vote. (McClure's, Seattle Public Library, via Wikimedia Commons)

By December 1910, Rankin had returned to Montana and became active in trying to help her own state give women the right to vote. In Washington, she had learned the benefits of grass-roots campaigning – meeting local people in small groups to talk about the issue. She started a group called the Political Equality Club of Missoula and began speaking out about the need for Montanans to grant women the right to vote. She was so impressive that she was invited to the state capital of Helena to speak to the state legislature. She was still only 30 years old at the time, and this was the first time a woman had been asked to address state lawmakers in Montana.

*Jeannette Rankin holding a suffrage flag while campaigning
for women's right to vote in Montana.
(Montana Historical Society Research Center)*

She told legislators that it was unfair for women to have responsibilities raising children and working, yet having no say in the conditions surrounding either.

"It's beautiful and right that a woman should nurse her sick children through typhoid fever, but it's also beautiful and right that she should vote for sanitary measures to prevent that typhoid from spreading," she told lawmakers.

Although the suffrage proposal did not pass in Montana at this time, the word about Jeannette Rankin was spreading.

A leading suffragette

Over the next five years, Rankin would become one of the leading suffrage voices in America. She was in demand around the country, as women in state after state pushed to get women the right to vote.

On March 25, 1911, tragedy occurred in New York City when 146 women working in a factory died in what became known as the Triangle Shirtwaist Fire. Protest marches in New York demanded the end of unsafe working conditions for women. This disaster gave momentum to the suffrage movement.

Protest marchers after the Triangle Shirtwaist Fire in New York City in 1911 killed 146 women. This tragedy helped the suffrage movement. (U.S. National Archives, via Wikimedia Commons)

"Women need votes to end sweatshops," a marcher's banner proclaimed in 1911. Rankin was in New York working for suffrage at the time, walking the crowded tenement streets of the city, urging residents to give women the vote.

From New York, Rankin crisscrossed the country by train, car and stagecoach, to California, back to New York, to Ohio, Montana, North Dakota, Michigan and Florida, speaking to factory workers, housewives, miners and farmers – all in the name of suffrage.

She's "one of the best schooled and enthusiastic suffragettes to be found in America," a Florida newspaper reported.

A suffrage rally in Washington, D.C., on March 3, 1913, urging the government to give women the vote. (Photo by George Grantham Bain, U.S. Library of Congress, via Wikimedia Commons)

The suffrage movement was gathering momentum. More and more women – and more and more men - realized that women deserved the right to vote.

On March 3, 1913, in Washington, D.C., on the day before Woodrow Wilson was inaugurated as president, a huge suffrage rally took place. Just a few months later, on July 31, 1913, Rankin participated in a second rally in Washington, led by a 72-car procession carrying state petitions demanding suffrage.

A suffrage car procession nearing Washington, D.C., on July 31, 1913, to present suffrage petitions to Congress. (Photo by W.R. Ross, Library of Congress, via Wikimedia Commons)

A second try at Montana suffrage

By 1914, this organizing and speaking experience paid off for Rankin. She returned yet again to Montana to push for suffrage. She organized thousands of women to canvass the huge state, the country's fourth largest. They had to convince men to give up their exclusive power - to give women the right to vote, not an easy task in any state. Rankin wrote letters, traveled from town to town, drove up and down one dirt road after another, reportedly giving 25 speeches in 25 days. She even spoke to children.

"Ask your fathers why they won't let your mothers vote," she would tell them.

Montana suffrage workers, circa 1914. (Montana Historical Society Research Center)

With her passion for suffrage, Rankin had become a captivating public speaker.

"When Miss Rankin came forward to speak the air became electric," a colleague said later. "Young, attractive, energetic and glowing with friendliness and reason, Jeannette Rankin commanded attention as soon as she spoke."

However, Rankin was human. She worked so hard that one day she let her passion and emotion get the best of her. At suffrage headquarters in Butte, Montana, she got angry at someone or something and threw a fit, screaming at suffrage colleagues and throwing things in the office.

A colleague wrote to her, urging her to remain calm despite the "intense" pressure to succeed. Rankin seemed to have learned from her mistake. Although she had the reputation of being demanding with strong opinions, there were no other reported incidents of her losing her temper in such a violent way.

On Election Day, November 3, 1914, Montana became the 10th state to grant women the right to vote. The total was 41,301 votes for, 37,588 votes against. Rankin, as the leader of the suffrage movement in Montana, was now famous in the state.

Woman Suffrage

Is the Only Constitutional Amendment to be Voted on Nov. 3

VOTE "YES"

Because: 1 Taxation without representation is tyranny.
2 All governments derive their just powers from the consent of the governed.
3 The home demands it.
4 The worker needs it.

SAMPLE BALLOT.

☐ FOR the amendment to the constitution relating to the right of suffrage and the qualifications to hold office.

☐ Against the amendment to the constitution relating to the right of suffrage and the qualifications to hold office.

The suffrage ballot in Montana for November 3, 1914.
(The Suffrage Daily News, via Montanawomenshistory.org)

She saw this movement as a way to improve living, working and health conditions for men, women and children. And soon she realized she was ready to take the next step.

Chapter 5: Breaking a Barrier in America

Jeannette Rankin's 1916 campaign photo.
(Montana Historical Society Research Center)

Sometimes in life, success comes from having a little luck on your side.

In 1915 and 1916, Rankin was thinking of running for

the United States Congress. No other woman had ever been elected to serve in the House of Representatives. Rankin knew she had a difficult task ahead. Yet she was forever the optimist, always confident that she could succeed. Her younger brother, Wellington, by now a successful Montana lawyer, said he would offer financial support and act as her campaign manager. Her four sisters (a fifth sister had died as a child), all successful in their own right, agreed to help her campaign.

Jeannette Rankin and her brother, Wellington, around the time she ran for Congress. He supported her and helped finance her campaign. (Montana Historical Society Research Center)

As it happens, a quirk in the 1916 election rules in Montana would help Rankin. At the time, Montana would elect two members of Congress, but both would be elected statewide, not from two separate districts within the state, as would become custom later. So Rankin realized that if she came in first, *or second*, she would be elected.

On July 13, 1916, Rankin announced her candidacy for the Republican nomination for Congress.

"The primal motive for my seeking a seat in the national Congress is to further the suffrage work and to aid in every possible way the movement for nationwide suffrage, which will not cease until it is won," she said at the time.

Jeannette Rankin, standing in car, campaigned directly to the people across Montana.
(Montana Historical Society Research Center)

She also supported an eight-hour workday for women and laws to improve the life and health of children, known as child welfare laws.

Women by the thousands across Montana registered to vote. Rankin, by now with vast experience traveling and speaking, took to the roads to campaign, from factories to farms, to rail yards to mines to street corners.

"There are hundreds of men [in Congress] to care for the nation's tariffs and foreign policy and irrigation projects," she said on the campaign trail. "But there isn't a single woman to look after the nation's greatest asset: its children."

The harder she campaigned, the more momentum she gained. A statewide Jeannette Rankin day was called.

A headline in a local newspaper said:

Brass Bands Greet Jeannette Rankin All over the State

On August 29, 1916, Rankin won the Republican nomination with 22,549 votes – 7,080 more than the closest of seven men who ran against her.

Now, it was on to the general election.

On November 6, 1916, Rankin had the opportunity to vote for the first time in her life in a main election – and she voted for herself. So did lots of other people. Remember, she only had to finish first or second in this general election to get elected to Congress.

The first reports were that Rankin had lost. It often took

days to count all the votes in far off rural areas, and the communication in those years was slow, with no radio or TV.

On the night of November 6, Rankin called the local newspaper and asked who won. She was told she had lost.

On November 7, the newspapers reported that she had, in fact, lost the election.

It was not until four days after the election, after all the vote totals had been counted, that it was determined Rankin came in second. With 76,932 votes (7,567 votes behind the winner and 6,354 votes ahead of the third place finisher), Jeannette Rankin had become the first woman elected to Congress. She was 36 years old and now, perhaps, the most famous woman in America.

When she was elected to Congress in 1916, Jeannette Rankin instantly became a national celebrity. (Library of Congress, via Wikimedia Commons)

"Why – Jeannette Rankin – you have given Suffrage the biggest push forward that could have possibly been given unless we could have elected a woman president," a supporter wrote.

Rankin was overwhelmed by press coverage – and given the period in our history, much of the coverage was extremely sexist by today's standards.

Newspapers reported on Rankin's hair color and dress and her dancing, sewing and cooking skills. One publication even called her the "maid of Missoula." She received marriage proposals through the mail. As a national celebrity, a toothpaste company offered her $5,000 to use her smiling photograph for an ad. She was in such demand that she was paid $500 per speech.

Rankin always seemed calm and confident: "I'm not nervous about going to Congress," she said, explaining that her social work "… gave me insight into the needs of babies, children and young adults, and it is for them that I shall work."

Chapter 6: Jeannette Rankin's Vote on a World Stage

After being elected, Congresswoman Jeannette Rankin had tremendous responsibility - and the world was watching. (Montana Historical Society Research Center)

Along with national and international fame for Jeannette Rankin, came much greater responsibility. She no longer was just that pioneering suffragette from Montana. As a member of Congress, she now had the obligation to focus on issues of international importance.

In 1914, World War I had begun in Europe. Germany, Austria and the other Central Powers in Europe were trying to conquer much of Europe, including Britain, France, Russia and Italy. President Woodrow Wilson had vowed to keep the United States out of war, but then events began to draw the United States closer to conflict.

The passenger ship Lusitania, as shown in this painting, was attacked and sunk by a German submarine on May 7, 1915. This was a turning point in U.S. international relations. (German Federal Archives, via Wikimedia Commons)

In May 1915, a German submarine torpedoed and sank the Lusitania, a British ocean liner sailing from New York to Liverpool, England. More than 1,100 passengers died, including 120 Americans. The attack was front-page international news. It later became known that this civilian ship was carrying American war materials for Britain. Although relations between the U.S. and Germany calmed for a period, in March 1917, German ships sank four U.S. merchant ships. The public mood in the U.S. had shifted. War was in the air.

President Wilson called an emergency meeting of Congress for April 2, 1917. This would be Jeannette Rankin's first day in the Capitol as a member of Congress.

Jeannette Rankin speaking to supporters, just before going to the Capitol on her first official day as a congresswoman in Washington, on April 2, 1917. (Photo by C.T. Chapman, Library of Congress, via Wikimedia Commons)

The day began on a high note for Rankin. She was honored by suffragists and other supporters at a breakfast. A wonderful picture was taken of her smiling at and speaking to supporters from the balcony of the National American Woman Suffrage Association.

She was about to make history. She was handed a bouquet of flowers and then driven down Pennsylvania Avenue to the Capitol in an open car, waving to supporters as she was escorted by 25-flag draped cars.

Congresswoman Rankin about to be driven to the Capitol on her first day in Congress. (National Photo Company Collection, Library of Congress, via Wikimedia Commons)

Washington's streets were crowded and noisy that day - filled with Rankin supporters, as well as those who were pro and anti-war.

Rankin's anti-war sentiments were well known, but many

in her suffrage movement urged her to support war, fearing an anti-war vote would kill the suffrage movement.

At a little after noon on that day, Rankin became the first woman to enter Congress as a member. The full House of Representatives – all men – rose and applauded as she walked into the chamber, carrying the purple, white and yellow flowers, the colors of the women's suffrage movement. With great pride, her mother and brother observed from the visitor's gallery.

President Wilson addresses Congress

Later that evening, President Wilson entered the chamber to make one of the most important speeches in U.S. history.

President Woodrow Wilson asking Congress to declare war on Germany, April 2, 1917. (Library of Congress, via Wikimedia Commons)

It was a solemn occasion. Most in attendance knew there was a great chance the president would ask for a declaration of war. The president said Germany's submarine warfare, its attacking of U.S. ships, was an act of war that could no longer be tolerated. He said the United States must be a champion of peace and freedom. "The world must be made safe for democracy," he said, in words that became famous.

He spoke for a little more than 20 minutes. Then he departed from the Capitol and left it to Congress to vote for or against war. The mood in the country had shifted from a few years ago – from one of remaining neutral to wanting to protect our liberties after being attacked at sea.

German soldiers fighting in France in 1914 during World War I. There was great pressure on Congresswoman Rankin and other members of Congress to vote for the U.S. to enter the war. (Photo by the German Army, via Wikimedia Commons)

Yes, Rankin was an avowed pacifist. She opposed war unless the United States was attacked on its own soil. But there was intense pressure on her to vote for war.

Many suffragettes thought Rankin needed to support the resolution, so as not to hurt the women's suffrage movement. Her brother urged her to vote yes, so as not to jeopardize her career. "Vote a man's vote," he reportedly told her. Friends and colleagues gathered in her Capitol office to pressure her to vote one way or the other. The House debated the issue. Most speakers supported joining the war.

Finally, the roll call vote began. Members of Congress would vote yes or no. On the first roll call, the clerk read the names one by one, alphabetically. No doubt, Rankin was nervous. This was not only her first vote in Congress, but the first vote by a woman in the history of Congress, dating back to 1789, when Congress first voted. As was her right, Rankin chose not to vote in the first roll call. She could wait for the second vote. Clearly, Rankin was feeling intense pressure, perhaps even some indecision. For years, she had argued that international wars did not solve international problems. She said wars were often the result of greed and the desire for individuals and countries to make money by selling weapons.

When Rankin's name was called during the second roll call, she stood up and spoke: "I want to stand by my country, but I cannot vote for war. I vote no." That was it. The first vote ever by a woman in the United States Congress was a vote against war. The war declaration passed 373 to 50. Although Rankin joined 49 congressmen in voting against war, it is clear from history that Rankin was the one who was criticized the most.

Congresswoman Rankin voted against the U.S. entering WW I. Despite press reports, it is unclear if she really sobbed. (The Daily Missoulian, courtesy Jeannette Rankin Peace Center)

She was attacked nationally for the vote. A Montana newspaper called her "… a member of the [German] army in the United States."

A leading suffragette wrote: "Our Congress Lady is sure enough a joker. Whatever she has done or will do… she loses us a million votes."

But there was support, too. The *Helena Independent* newspaper wrote: "Montana's Congresswoman is Now Very Popular… Her mind is honest and open and she has evident courage to back her convictions."

Although there is no verified proof to this, some newspapers reported that she cried when delivering her vote.

She did not care that her vote may have doomed her political career.

"Never for one second could I face the idea that I would send your men to be killed for no other reason than to save my seat in Congress," she said later.

In a later photo, Jeannette Rankin with some of the congressmen who joined her in voting against war in April 1917. (National Council for Prevention of War Records, Photograph Collection, Swarthmore College Peace Collection)

Within a day, the war declaration was signed by President Wilson. Eventually, the United States and its allies would win the war, but more than 300,000 U.S. soldiers would die or be injured in the fighting.

Although her term in Congress was just starting, this vote was her defining moment, a vote she would be remembered for throughout history. She certainly wanted America to win the war. She focused her attention on women's and children's rights – in the home and in the work place - issues that were always very important to her. She introduced bills in Congress. All these efforts failed at the time.

But there was one issue where Rankin was asked by the men of Congress for leadership.

Chapter 7: The Suffrage Movement in Congress

Congresswoman Rankin, right, during a suffrage event in Washington, circa 1917. (Library of Congress, via Wikimedia Commons)

In the summer of 1917, the push began to convince President Wilson and Congress to give women the right to vote on a national level – so they could vote in presidential elections.

Rankin was asked to take the lead in Congress. On January 10, 1918, Rankin addressed the full Congress. The House and the Senate would have to pass a resolution for a constitutional amendment and then three-quarters of the states would need to ratify the amendment for it to become the law.

Congresswoman Rankin making her first speech to Congress in 1917. In 1918, she addressed Congress and asked that women be given the right to vote. (Wikimedia Commons)

"We as a nation were born in a land of unparalleled resources… But something is still lacking," Rankin told Congress. "… babies are dying from cold and hunger and soldiers have died for lack of a woolen shirt. Might it not be that men who have spent their lives thinking in terms of commercial profit find it hard to adjust themselves to thinking in terms of human needs?

"Is it not possible that the women of the country have something of value to give the nation at this time? … We declared war not state by state but by federal action… How shall we explain… the meaning of democracy if the same Congress that voted for war to make the world safe for democracy refuses to give this small measure of democracy to the women of our country?"

The resolution for women's suffrage passed in the House of Representatives by 274-136. But the resolution did not pass the Senate and it died that year in Congress. Yet momentum was building.

Rankin's no vote for war had made her less popular. She served only one two-year term in Congress. She tried to run for the Senate, but was defeated.

Jeannette Rankin's public life was over, for now. She had made a tremendous impact. Women (and many men) across the country and world admired her. A woman had finally been elected to Congress. In July 1917, a Connecticut newspaper reported that because of Rankin, more and more parents were naming their newborn girls Jeannette. In fact, statistics show this was true. From 1900 to 1910, Jeannette was not among the 200 most popular girls' names in the country. But the next decade, during her rise to fame, the name Jeannette joined the list at #186. There were 7,719 little Jeannette's across the country – far more than in the previous decade.

In 1919, after Rankin left office, Congress voted to approve the constitutional amendment that would give women the right to vote. This was certainly partly due to Rankin's efforts when she was in Congress. As a final step, three quarters of the states had to approve, or ratify, the constitutional amendment to change the law. A year later, in the summer of 1920, Tennessee became the 36th state to ratify the 19th Amendment to the U.S. Constitution – giving women the right to vote.

Women voting after the 19th Amendment was passed granting women the right to vote across the country. (Library of Congress, via Bustle.com)

Chapter 8: The Fight for Peace Continues After Congress

Although Rankin was retired from Congress by 1919, she was only 39 years old and was hardly the retiring type. She had too much energy, too much to say and too much influence to just sit back and relax and live a quiet, country life in Montana. She knew she had to be involved in and speak out about the important issues she believed in.

Soon after leaving Congress, she attended the Women's International League for Peace and Freedom in Europe, with many important women's rights activists. They visited battlefields and cemeteries in France from World War I. They saw the horrors of war up close. They sent suggestions to President Wilson for the peace treaty that ended WW I. Their suggestions were rejected, but seeing the devastation from years of fighting strengthened Rankin's desire for worldwide peace. She saw it as her mission.

"The work of educating the world for peace is a woman's job, because men are afraid of being classed as cowards if they oppose war," she would say later.

For the next 20 years, Rankin was a strong advocate for peace. She found a new base of operation.

A Belgian forest destroyed during World War I. Rankin visited Europe and viewed some of the battlefields. This reinforced her anti-war beliefs. (Australian War Memorial, via Wikimedia Commons)

She loved Montana, but while living in Washington, she had grown interested in the South. She liked the warm weather and wanted to be closer to Washington and to New York City.

In 1923, she paid $500 for a 64-acre farm near the small town of Bogart, Georgia, a short distance from the University of Georgia, an intellectual environment that Rankin thought might be receptive to her ideas about peace. She chose to live simply. The farm had a small cabin, with no kitchen, no bathroom, no running water and no electricity. She built a cooking area in an adjacent building and an outhouse.

Jeannette Rankin outside her home in Georgia in the 1920s.
(Montana Historical Society Research Center)

She used old, crumpled magazines "for toilet paper, and very rough paper it was, while all our neighbors wiped on catalogues with slick paper," a niece recalled.

She grew peaches, cherries, berries, plums, apples and figs and had 200 pecan trees. She made jellies and jams. She earned some money farming, but chose to live without luxuries, relying on a small inheritance and the kindness of her brother, Wellington, the attorney who had become a wealthy landowner in Montana. She loved her farm.

She "cherished her trees as some women cherish diamonds," a friend wrote. "She cleared away only the dead ones and woe to anybody who snapped a green branch or broke a living shoot. I think she knew by name every tree on her land."

Yet Rankin was not just a farmer. She established the Georgia Peace Society and began to speak out.

Speaking out for peace

As a former member of Congress, she still had influence in Washington. Organizations that shared her beliefs hired her as a lobbyist to try to convince congressmen and senators to pass laws they wanted. One organization hired her to lobby for improved maternal and infant care, for safer factory worker conditions, for a minimum wage, and for protections against child labor.

Men lined up outside a soup kitchen in Chicago during the Depression. During this difficult time, Jeannette Rankin lobbied Congress to pass laws to improve the welfare of men, women and children. (U.S. National Archives, via Wikimedia Commons)

She took a job for $250 a month with the Women's International League for Peace and Freedom (WILPF). She traveled all over the East Coast and Midwest, speaking at colleges, luncheons and tea parties. She encouraged women to get involved in the peace movement.

"No woman can with honor ask her son to go to war unless she can say that she has done everything in her power to prevent the necessity of making such a sacrifice," she said in a speech in Dayton, Ohio.

But Rankin didn't last long at the WILPF. She quit after they could not pay for her staff.

During her time in Georgia, she became friendly with her neighbors and their children. She formed clubs to keep them busy and help them learn.

In 1929, she began a 10-year relationship with the National Council for the Prevention of War, for $150 a month. She traveled the country coast to coast, speaking about pacifist ways.

"She made all preparations for war seem so absolutely silly and nonsensical that one wonders why we keep it up at all," wrote one pastor in Washington state.

One college in Georgia even suggested it might make Jeannette Rankin a professor of "peace."

But Rankin had her foes. A Georgia newspaper called Rankin a "communist," stating, "Up pops the devil." Rankin could accept criticism, but not if it spread lies about her. She sued the newspaper for libel. The newspaper apologized and settled the case for $1,000.

Jeannette Rankin meeting with Senator Gerald Nye in Washington in 1935, as she continued to push her pacifist beliefs. (Montana Historical Society Research Center)

War on the horizon

By 1935, the tides of history were again swinging towards world war. Italy was fighting in Ethiopia. The Spanish Civil War was underway. Japan was fighting China. And Adolph Hitler and the Nazis were firmly in power in Germany, and building a war machine.

Italian soldiers fighting in Ethiopia in 1935. The winds of war were blowing against Rankin's pacifists beliefs. (Library of Congress, via Wikimedia Commons)

Rankin gave hundreds of speeches over the next couple of years. She warned that American and international businesses had a motive for going to war, because they made a lot of money – known as war profiteering. She warned that war would destroy democracy. She met with Eleanor Roosevelt, President Franklin Roosevelt's wife, to urge her to promote peace. And she testified before Congress, arguing that the U.S. should only protect its own borders, and should remain neutral in Europe and Asia.

She spoke her famous line about the futility of war: "You can no more win a war than you can an earthquake."

Yet history again was not on Jeannette Rankin's side.

Chapter 9: History Repeats Itself

German troops march through Warsaw, Poland, after they invaded the country in 1939. (U.S. National Archives, via Wikimedia Commons)

On September 1, 1939, Germany invaded Poland. Two days later, Britain and France declared war on Germany. World War II was underway. Although the United States would not enter the war for more than two years, the world now had changed, and so had America.

As the war escalated in Europe, more and more Americans sensed the U.S. might have to join the fight. The government increased its spending on the military. Pacifists – and pacifism – were becoming less popular.

Of course, this change would not stop Rankin. In fact, it made her more determined. She had left Congress 20 years before. Rankin was now almost 60, no longer the young woman who startled America by becoming the first woman elected to Congress. She began thinking that the best way to keep America neutral and out of World War II was to speak from a powerful perch as a U.S. congresswoman. She decided to run for Congress again from Montana.

Jeannette Rankin's campaign photograph from 1940. She ran for a second term on a peace platform. (Montana Historical Society Research Center)

She chose an unusual campaign strategy. She decided to appeal to a younger generation. She wrote to or called all 56 high schools in her congressional district. She informed the schools she would arrive on a certain date. But she did not provide her own contact info, so the schools could not cancel. She drove herself from school to school and spoke her mind.

"Talk to your parents. Tell them to write to the president that they don't want this country to go to war again," she said.

She also urged students to write to the president and teased the boys that girls were rising in society. "Someday, one of you may be the husband of a president," she said.

By July 1940, Europe was engulfed in war. Germany had already invaded Czechoslovakia, Denmark, Norway, Holland, Belgium and Poland. Italy was fighting on the side of Germany. French and British troops were engaged in battle with the Nazis. And the Germans were bombing London and other locations in England in what became known as the Battle of Britain.

America at the time was torn. There were strong arguments for war and strong arguments against it. It was a bitter and angry public feud between the two sides. Some people who opposed the U.S. entering war were considered anti-American and pro-German. President Roosevelt, seeing the violent news from Europe, was preparing the country for war.

Firefighters putting out a fire in London after a German bombing attack. (U.S. National Archives, via Wikimedia Commons)

But Rankin's campaign slogan was clear:

Prepare to the limit for defense.

Keep our men out of Europe.

Dozens of women worked for Rankin's campaign, traveling the state, speaking out on her behalf at meetings and on radio.

No mistake about it - she was running on a peace platform. "By voting for me… you can express your opposition to sending your son to foreign lands to fighting a foreign war and by voting for me you will also express your determination to prepare to the absolute limit to defend this country."

She won the Republican primary. On November 5, 1940, she won the general election by more than 9,000 votes with a 56,616 vote total. She no longer was a national novelty. She would join 10 other women in Congress. The potential for war and the national defense were the dominant issues.

Rankin made several proposals in Congress to help keep America out of the war. She proposed making it more difficult for the president and Congress to send U.S. soldiers overseas to fight, and she proposed making it more difficult for the government to budget money for war.

"I am still trying to keep our men from being sacrificed in the slaughter house across the ocean," she wrote to a friend.

Her proposals were defeated.

By the fall of 1941, as the newspapers reported on the spread of war across Europe – Germany had now invaded Russia - American opinions began to change. Rankin was still urging America to stay out of war and to find a diplomatic solution.

Then one of the worst days in U.S. history occurred.

The attack on Pearl Harbor changes the course of history
On Sunday, December 7, 1941, at 7:40 in the morning, a Japanese Navy commander sent a coded message to Japanese pilots flying over the Pacific. This would begin the Japanese

bombing attack on the U.S. Navy in Pearl Harbor, Hawaii. A total of 353 airplanes that had been launched from Japanese aircraft carriers carried out the attack – an attack that would be the worst military assault ever against the United States.

Japan's attack on the U.S. Navy at Pearl Harbor on December 7, 1941, was the single worst attack ever against the U.S. military, killing more than 2,400 sailors. (U.S. National Archives, via Wikimedia Commons)

It was devastating for the American Pacific fleet. More than 2,400 U.S. sailors were killed and almost 1,300 were wounded. A total of 19 U.S. Navy ships were sunk or damaged.

Rankin and her sister Edna were at home in Rankin's

apartment in Washington when they heard the news on the radio. Rankin could not believe such a tragedy had occurred. No one could. Still in shock, Rankin boarded a train that evening for Detroit because of a prior speaking engagement, but then she rushed back to Washington because President Roosevelt announced he would address a joint session of Congress the next day at noon.

The nation was shocked by Japan's attack on Pearl Harbor. (The Boston Daily Globe)

Upon returning to Washington the next morning, Rankin tried to take a nap, when her brother, Wellington, called. He pleaded with her to vote for war to protect her political future. But her political future was not on her mind, because that's not the way Rankin thought. She left her house and drove for hours so she could be alone and think. She didn't want to talk with anyone at the time. She knew many people would pressure her to vote for war, because after Pearl Harbor, the country's mood was overwhelmingly in support of America joining the fight.

"I got into my car and left the office… [N]o one knew where I was. And no one could get after me; no one could bring any pressure on me, because I knew what I was going to do," she said later.

At about noon on December 8, President Roosevelt was driven to the Capitol from the White House in his 1928 bullet proof Cadillac. He had written and rewritten his speech, a speech, like President Woodrow Wilson's before WW I, which would go down in American history as one of the nation's most important.

At approximately 12:30 pm, the president, unable to walk on his own, was helped to the podium. The Capitol's congressional chamber was packed with senators, members of the House of Representatives, congressional staffers, the press and scores of observers, much as it was 24 years earlier when President Wilson delivered his address.

President Franklin Roosevelt delivering his address to Congress on December 8, 1941. He asked for a declaration of war against Japan. (U.S. National Archives, via Wikimedia Commons)

"Yesterday, December 7, 1941, a date which will live in infamy, the United States of America was suddenly and deliberately attacked," President Roosevelt began. These words echoed across America, as almost every family listened to the speech on the radio. He asked Congress to declare war on Japan.

Jeannette Rankin, now a gray-haired, middle-aged woman, sat and listened to this speech. A woman who had devoted years of her life to spreading and encouraging pacifism, she heard the loud applause around her as the president said, "I believe that I interpret the will of the Congress and of the people when I assert that we will not only defend ourselves to the uttermost, but will make it very certain that this form of treachery shall never again endanger us."

After President Roosevelt spoke, the House of Representatives and the Senate, separately, had to consider a declaration of war. In the House, there was little discussion. Within 18 minutes, members moved for a vote. Rankin no doubt felt intense pressure. She shouted: "Mr. Speaker, I object." The speaker of the House silenced her by saying, "You're out of order."

One congressman after another rose to speak in support of going to war with Japan. Rankin tried to stop a vote. She stood and waved, but the House speaker ignored her. She tried again… and again.

"Mr. Speaker! I would like to be heard!" she shouted.

She was ignored. A radio reporter said: "Miss Rankin is on her feet. She's asking to be heard."

The Senate had voted for war by an 82-0 vote. The House vote began as they went alphabetically through the members. One vote after another for war. When they got to Rankin, she shouted, "As a woman, I can't go to war and I refuse to send anyone else." The vote went on until the end.

In the World War I vote, 49 men had joined Rankin in voting no. This time she stood alone. The final vote: 388 for war, 1 against. Rankin was the only member of Congress to vote against the U.S. entering World War II. She was booed in the Congressional chamber and even worse outside of it. People called her a traitor.

After the vote, she was harassed by people in the Capitol

building, who couldn't imagine that a person could vote no for war after the Pearl Harbor attack. She ducked into a phone booth to call the Capitol Police for help.

Congresswoman Rankin in a phone booth calling Capitol Police for assistance, after being harassed for voting against war. (Bettmann, Getty Images)

She said she had no choice but to vote against war, because she was against it and had campaigned on that position.

Her brother, Wellington, said in a phone call later that day: "Montana is 110 percent against you."

After the vote, Rankin released a statement to the press: "When I cast the only vote against war, I remembered the promises I had made during my campaign for election to do everything possible to keep this country out of war," she said.

"I was thinking of the pledges I had made to the mothers and fathers of Montana that I would do all in my power to prevent their sons being slaughtered on foreign battlefields." (*See Rankin's entire statement at the end of the book.*)

Rankin's office was flooded with angry, nasty letters.

"You made an ass out of yourself trying to be like a man."

"I hope a Jap bomb drops on your head or home."*

Rankin was called a "petty-coated idiot."

"Resign, you poor sissy."

The *Daily News* in Eugene, Oregon, wrote: "Either Miss Rankin is stupid or emotionally unsound. In either case she does not belong in the House of Representatives."

*

Congresswoman Rankin's no vote against the U.S. joining WW II on Dec. 8, 1941, angered many people. (The Washington Daily News, Courtesy of Jeannette Rankin Peace Center)

*** "Japs" or "Jap" were derogatory terms used during World War II referring to Japan and the Japanese people. These words are considered highly offensive today.**

The letters went on and on, attacking her intelligence, her patriotism (she was accused of having an agreement with Hitler), her ability as a woman to be a member of Congress.

"She dismissed the bombing as lightly as she would a run in her stocking," one newspaper columnist wrote.

But there were many letters of support, too.

One supporter wrote that Rankin's vote will be appreciated once Americans start dying on foreign battlefields.

A Montanan wrote: "In all of history no man has done so brave, so commendable a thing … Today, I feel that you've vindicated womanhood."

The Emporia Gazette in Kansas wrote: "Well – look at Jeannette Rankin. Probably a hundred men in Congress would like to do what she did. Not one of them had the courage to do it."

In 1942, with the U.S. war effort in high gear, Rankin decided she would not run for re-election. She accomplished little in Congress during her two-year term. Clearly, her pacifist philosophy was not in tune with America.

"Jeannette was completely out of step with the times and she knew it," biographer Norma Smith wrote in *Jeannette Rankin: America's Conscience*.

Despite all the criticism, Jeannette Rankin left behind further proof that she was not afraid to speak her mind, no matter how much public opinion was against her. Just before she left Congress in early 1943, Rankin took a parting shot at President Roosevelt and all the other political leaders who took America to war.

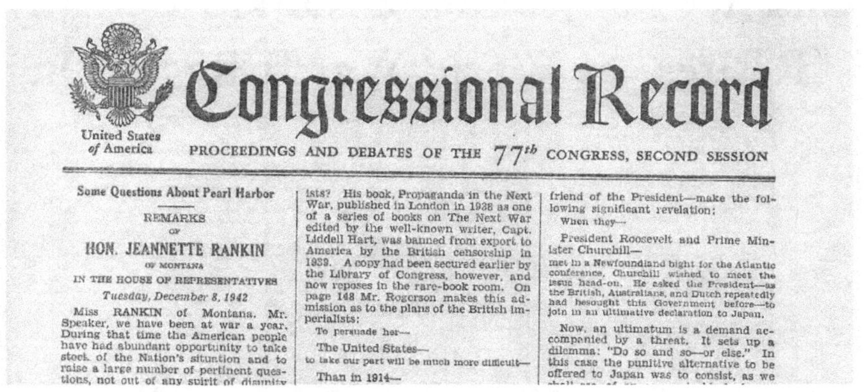

Congressional Record

United States of America — PROCEEDINGS AND DEBATES OF THE 77th CONGRESS, SECOND SESSION

Some Questions About Pearl Harbor

REMARKS
OF
HON. JEANNETTE RANKIN
OF MONTANA

IN THE HOUSE OF REPRESENTATIVES

Tuesday, December 8, 1942

Miss RANKIN of Montana. Mr. Speaker, we have been at war a year. During that time the American people have had abundant opportunity to take stock of the Nation's situation and to raise a large number of pertinent questions, not out of any spirit of disunity

ists? His book, Propaganda in the Next War, published in London in 1938 as one of a series of books on The Next War edited by the well-known writer, Capt. Liddell Hart, was banned from export to America by the British censorship in 1939. A copy had been secured earlier by the Library of Congress, however, and now reposes in the rare-book room. On page 148 Mr. Rogerson makes this admission as to the plans of the British imperialists:

To persuade her—

The United States—

to take our part will be much more difficult—

Than in 1914—

friend of the President—make the following significant revelation:

When they—

President Roosevelt and Prime Minister Churchill—

met in a Newfoundland bight for the Atlantic conference. Churchill wished to meet the issue head-on. He asked the President—as the British, Australians, and Dutch repeatedly had besought this Government before—to join in an ultimative declaration to Japan.

Now, an ultimatum is a demand accompanied by a threat. It sets up a dilemma: "Do so and so—or else." In this case the punitive alternative to be offered to Japan was to consist, as we

Congresswoman Rankin published a long statement in the Congressional Record on Dec. 8, 1942, questioning why the U.S. entered WW II. (Congressional Record, Dec. 8, 1942)

Rankin published a long statement in the *Congressional Record*, a written journal of events that take place in Congress. She claimed that Roosevelt and Winston Churchill, Britain's leader, conspired to provoke Japan into attacking the United States by stopping the sale of raw materials to Japan. She said the United States knew it would be attacked.

"…[W]hy did the President permit our forces at Pearl Harbor to be taken by surprise?" she wrote. Rankin's conspiracy theory, written about by many, has been controversial over the years and has received some support. However, it has not been widely accepted.

Chapter 10: Jeannette Rankin Actually "Retires" as World War II Rages On

Stalingrad, Russia, in 1943, after a long battle for the city. The world's attention was on WW II, drowning out Rankin's voice for peace. (RIA Novosti Archive, via Wikimedia Commons)

By 1943, Jeannette Rankin was 62 years old and realized her public life was over. She could not get re-elected again. And the peace movement, her life-long passion, was dead for now, because America was fighting for freedom in Europe, in the biggest war the world had ever known.

Rankin returned to Georgia and built a new home called

Shady Grove, after her original home burned down. She got to know her neighbors, some of whom were quite poor. She built a home for them on her property and they helped her on her land. She also spent time in Montana, caring for her sick, elderly mother.

By the time World War II ended, in 1945, Rankin decided she wanted to explore the world, particularly India. She was a big supporter of the Indian leader Mahatma Gandhi, who helped India gain independence. She studied Gandhi's non-violent ways, his methods of passive resistance to authority.

Mahatma Gandhi's pacifist beliefs and non-violent protests in India influenced Jeannette Rankin. She traveled to India seven times. (Wikimedia Commons)

Gandhi "used spiritual power," not violence, to solve

political problems, Rankin said. She would go to India seven times over the course of two decades to live, study and meet leaders and average people throughout the country.

Jeannette Rankin traveling in India during one of her many visits to the country.
(Montana Historical Society Research Center)

But Gandhi's and Rankin's pacifist beliefs were not the norm. In 1945, the United States ended World War II by dropping two atomic bombs on Japan – bombs that killed more than 100,000 people. By 1949, the Soviet Union would test its first nuclear weapon. The nuclear arms race and the Cold War between the United States and Russia were underway.

Rankin saw the world differently. She supported Gandhi's principle of total world disarmament. She never met Gandhi, because he was assassinated in 1948, but his beliefs certainly lived on in her mind.

Exploring the world

In addition to visiting India, Rankin toured South Africa, South America, Iran, Turkey, Ireland, Europe, Hawaii, Egypt, Indo-China and Russia.

Rankin visiting the pyramids during a trip to Egypt. Although she went sightseeing, Rankin traveled mostly to learn about people and countries that were different from what she knew. (Montana Historical Society Research Center)

Wherever she went, she wanted to learn: "I have not come to Iran to talk," she said, "but to discover how people live and the condition of women in Iran and what they are thinking about world conditions and the problems that concern us all."

She urged the Russians at a world peace conference to unilaterally disarm. "Why talk about it? Just disarm," she said.

Although mostly out of public life, Rankin was still one of the most respected and famous women in America. In 1958, Sen. John F. Kennedy, before he became president, wrote an article in *McCall's Magazine* praising three women for their courage – one of them was Rankin.

Although Rankin traveled extensively, she spent much of these years on her Georgia farm, out of the spotlight. She continued to have little interest in material possessions. Biographer Kevin S. Giles reported in *One Woman Against War: The Jeannette Rankin Story* that she rejected offers to live in a fully modern house. Her farm in Georgia had floors covered with plastic, tarpaper and Oriental rugs. She pumped water from a nearby well. One table was an old orange crate. Electric wires ran across a room. She had no indoor plumbing and when she needed heat, she burned old copies of *The New York Times* in the fireplace.

Jeannette Rankin, in a later photo, re-entered public life in her 80s as an anti-war activist opposing U.S. fighting in the Vietnam War. (Montana Historical Society Research Center)

By 1965, Rankin had been mostly absent from public life for more than 20 years. She was now 85 years old, an age when few people would embark on a new, public action. But Rankin still had the fire to speak out. As America's involvement in the Vietnam War began to increase, and public opposition to the war grew, Rankin would re-enter public life as a respected elder statesman. Her beliefs as a pacifist were no longer just held by a few. America had come full circle: From fighting in World War II, in a war that almost all Americans believed was essential to securing peace and democracy worldwide, to now fighting in a war that would become America's least popular foreign war in history.

Chapter 11: Jeannette Rankin, An Anti-War Activist at Age 86

Dr. Martin Luther King Jr. on the steps of the Lincoln Memorial the day he delivered his "I Have a Dream" speech in August 1963. The 1960s was a period of great turmoil and change in America. (Wikimedia Commons)

The 1960s was a time of great turmoil in the United States and elsewhere. This was a period of civil unrest, violence and also exciting change. Dr. Martin Luther King Jr. and others were fighting and dying for civil rights. Young people began to speak out like never before about their beliefs, challenging authority and our country's leaders.

It also was a time when women began to form independent movements. Women's liberation and the feminist movement began to take shape. A new organization called the National Organization of Women (NOW) unveiled a plan that had strong similarities to beliefs expressed by Jeannette Rankin decades before, beliefs about women's rights and the rights of children.

In 1917 and in 1941, Rankin had stood alone as a congresswoman on a national stage shouting out for peace. By the mid-1960s, as anti-war sentiment rose in America, Rankin no longer would stand alone.

By 1966, the U.S. fighting in the Vietnam War had increased considerably. Here, two soldiers await a helicopter to evacuate them and their comrade, who was killed in battle. (Photo by Pfc. L. Paul Epley, U.S. National Archives, Wikimedia Commons)

In 1966, more than 6,000 American soldiers would die in the Vietnam War, three times as many as the year before. Rankin took notice and could no longer remain silent. She placed an ad in eight Montana newspapers, urging voters to vote against congressional candidates if they did not oppose the war. Some newspapers rejected her ads. She asked to speak on an Atlanta TV station, but also was rejected.

In 1967, more than 11,000 U.S. soldiers would die in the Vietnam War, almost double from the year before. The anti-war movement was taking hold around the country. Thousands took to the streets in protest as young men burned their draft cards, to show they would not enter the military if drafted.

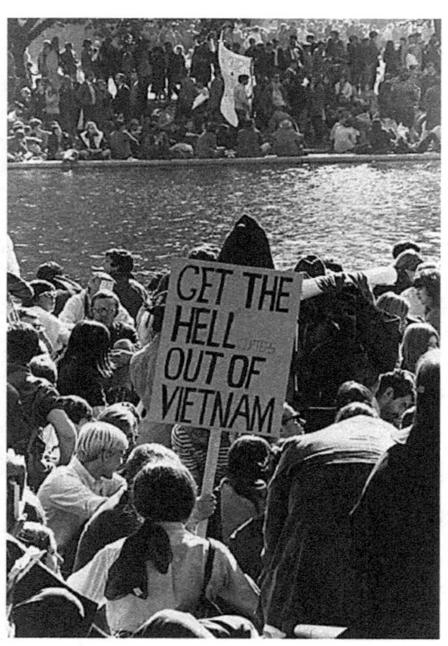

Vietnam War protestors in Washington, D.C., in 1967. The movement was led by a young generation, but this did not stop 86-year-old Jeannette Rankin from speaking out against the war. (Photo by Frank Wolfe, via Wikimedia Commons)

April 1967 was the 50th anniversary of Rankin's vote against World War I, and she received a lot of publicity.

"It isn't a question of war against Germany, Japan or Vietnam. It's just that the whole system is very stupid," she said. "War is nothing more than a method of settling a dispute, but it has nothing to do with the dispute. In fact, you never have the same issues at the end of war that were present at the beginning. Shooting a young man is no way to settle a political dispute."

In May of that year, Rankin was asked to address a small group of anti-war supporters at a home in Atlanta. She had not delivered a speech advocating peace in some 25 years. A reporter was present, so her words made headlines again.

Jeannette Rankin at a press conference with Coretta Scott King, Dr. Martin Luther King Jr.'s wife. They were speaking out against the Vietnam War, and they would march together to the Capitol as part of the Jeannette Rankin Brigade. (Bettmann, Getty Images)

"It is unconscionable that 10,000 boys have died in Vietnam [this year]," she said, "and I predict that if 10,000 American women had mind enough they could end the war, if they were committed to the task, even if it meant going to jail."

Rankin became a leading protestor against the Vietnam War. She was asked to lead a march on Washington. January 15, 1968, was opening day for the 90th Congress. It had snowed in Washington the night before and the streets were slushy as 5,000 women in the Jeannette Rankin Brigade marched to the Capitol. Enough young men had died in the war, they argued, for a war that would solve nothing. Marchers included Coretta Scott King, the wife of Dr. Martin Luther King Jr., members of the Black Panthers, senators' wives and ordinary women pushing strollers.

Jeannette Rankin, center with glasses, with Jeannette Rankin Brigade during 1968 march to the Capitol to protest U.S. fighting in the Vietnam War. (Getty Images)

*Jeannette Rankin Brigade button. (Mildred Scott Olmsted Papers: Button,
Pin and Ribbon Collection, Swarthmore College Peace Collection)*

Rankin and a small group of protestors presented a petition to congressional leaders calling for the end of the war. Rankin met with Senator Mike Mansfield to discuss her opposition to war.

As anti-war protests grew across America, Rankin gave newspaper and TV interviews, attacking the U.S. military as a threat to American democracy. At one such protest at the University of Georgia, Rankin told 1,500 students that the Vietnam War was being fought because American companies made money from it.

Jeannette Rankin meeting with Senator Mike Mansfield after the protest march to the Capitol by the Jeannette Rankin Brigade. (Montana Historical Society Research Center)

"We waste our money on the military," she said. "We spend over half of our peacetime money getting ready for the next war."

Rankin was greatly admired by this new generation of protestors. She was nearing her 90th birthday, participating in a peace movement lead by college kids, hippies and peaceniks.

Students across the country protested the Vietnam War. Above, a protest at Florida State University, Tallahassee, Florida, in 1970. (State Archives of Florida, Florida Memory, via Wikimedia Commons)

As the anti-war movement continued, Rankin is honored

Rankin continued to speak out against the Vietnam War despite her advanced age. On June 11, 1970, Rankin celebrated her 90th birthday with a dinner in her honor in Washington, D.C. Many famous politicians of the time attended.

Rankin is "ninety years young, tall as a giant in statesmanship that is unparalleled in American history," said Senator Margaret Chase Smith. "She broke the way for me by being elected in 1916. I salute her for being the original dove in Congress."

Congresswoman Rankin leaving the White House in 1917. Senators looked back on Rankin's career and praised her for being a groundbreaker and for standing up for what she believed in for 50 years. (Photo by Harris & Ewing, Library of Congress, via Wikimedia Commons)

Senator Lee Metcalf, from Rankin's home state of Montana, called Rankin one of the most prominent women in the world, fighting for peace, suffrage and women's and children's rights. She's a "saver with a great heart, a builder, a trailblazer and an example to all legislators who would have the courage of their convictions..."

Rankin stayed active close to the end of her life. Famous people sought her out. Gloria Steinem, the feminist leader, asked Rankin to appear with her on national TV. In comments to a reporter, Rankin said: "We must have absolutely unilateral disarmament" – meaning the U.S. must give up all its weapons, as an example for the world to follow.

In February 1972, Rankin received a huge honor in New York City, an honor that would cement her place as one of the leading women in 20th century American history. The National Organization for Women, perhaps the best-known women's rights organization in the country, made Rankin the first inductee into its Susan B. Anthony Hall of Fame. This was a fitting honor for Rankin. Fifty years before, Rankin was one of the leading suffrage leaders as states, then the federal government, granted women the right to vote. Susan B. Anthony is regarded as America's most famous suffrage leader.

Rankin received a prestigious award from the National Organization of Women on February 12, 1972, recognizing her as a leading feminist of the 20th century. (FPG, Hulton Archive, Getty Images)

With 1,500 people in attendance, Rankin was honored as "the world's outstanding living feminist."

In her acceptance speech, Rankin said: "Women must devote all their energies today in gaining enough political offices to influence the direction of government away from the military industrial complex and toward solving the major social disgraces that exist in our country. We are here together to work together for the elimination of war… my dream has always been that women would take this responsibility."

Chapter 12: One Last Issue

Jeannette Rankin had great passion and energy until near the end of her life. She was outspoken into her 90s. (U.S. Congress, via Wikimedia Commons)

In 1972, at the age of 92, Rankin even considered running for Congress again. But she realized this was impractical, because she was just too old to campaign effectively.

During this period, aside from the peace movement, Rankin had one other issue near and dear to her heart. Rankin believed that the Electoral College and the two-party system both should be abolished, to allow a more fair presidential election that better represented what people wanted. She believed the current system allowed the election of a president that did not accurately reflect who the people wanted to be president.

She supported voters having a broader group of candidates to choose from, to be elected by popular vote, not an Electoral College.

Her position has strong historical support. Five times in American history, including twice recently (2000 and 2016), the candidate who got the most popular votes was not elected president.

In the 2016 presidential election, Hillary Clinton received almost three million more votes than Donald Trump. (Photo by Lorie Shaull, via Wikimedia Commons)

In 2000, Al Gore received 500,000 more votes than George W. Bush, yet Bush became president.

In 2016, President Donald Trump defeated Hillary Clinton, even though Trump received almost three million fewer votes than Clinton.

Clinton was the first woman to receive a Democratic or Republican nomination to run for president. This came a full 100 years after Jeannette Rankin was the first woman elected to serve in Congress, the first woman able to stand and speak her mind in the halls of Congress as an elected official representing the federal government.

Whether in office, or out, Rankin argued for peace. Here, in 1939, she testified before a Congressional Committee against increased U.S. military spending. (Photo by Harris & Ewing, Library of Congress, via Wikimedia Commons)

Throughout her life, Rankin seemed to be inspired by something she wrote: "I believed then as I do now that women are the ones who must be concerned with the needs and development of the human race. I have always fought for the dignity of all human beings – for those of the present as well as those of future generations. I will continue to struggle as long as I live."

She followed that principal into old age, when the years finally caught up with her. In her last year in life, her health declined, she grew weak and lost the ability to speak. This would be hard for anyone, but perhaps particularly hard for Jeannette Rankin, a person who for 60 years had lived by her spoken words - her speeches, her interviews, her words of outrage in support of women's rights, women's suffrage and against war. Eventually, she became so frustrated that she asked her doctor to stop her medicines, so that she no longer would suffer through her old age. The doctor could not do this.

The statue of Jeannette Rankin in the Capitol, in Washington, D.C. (U.S. Capitol, via Wikimedia Commons)

Rankin is remembered as a great woman, a groundbreaking woman, a woman who set the path for many to come after her, but one who fought a losing battle for eternal peace on earth. She is remembered as a feminist ahead of her times, as a woman who never backed down, a woman who stood by her beliefs throughout her life.

Jeannette Rankin died of natural causes on May 18, 1973, in Carmel, California, a few weeks before she would have turned 93.

Jeannette Rankin Timeline

June 11, 1880: Jeannette Rankin was born on the family's ranch near Missoula, Montana.

1898: At age 18, Rankin graduates high school and enrolls at Montana State University in Missoula to study biology.

1902: Rankin graduates college.

1905: Rankin travels to Boston to care for her sick brother, Wellington, and for the first time observes poor immigrants suffering in the inner cities of Boston and New York.

1908: Rankin, age 28, travels to San Francisco and helps and learns about struggling immigrants; begins learning about laws designed to help protect women and children.

Later in 1908: Rankin moves to New York City to attend social work school.

1909: After social work school, Rankin moves to the state of Washington to work as a social worker, helping poor immigrants.

1910: Rankin enrolls in school in Washington state to study government; Discovers the suffrage movement and plays important role in helping women earn the right to vote in the state of Washington.

Late 1910: Rankin returns to Montana to help with state's suffrage movement. The movement fails at this time.

1911- 1914: Rankin becomes a leading suffrage advocate, working in states across the country helping women earn the right to vote.

1914: Rankin returns to Montana to help lead the state's suffrage movement as Montana becomes 10th state in the United States to grant women the right to vote.

July 13, 1916: Rankin announces her candidacy for U.S. Congress.

November 6, 1916: At age 36, Rankin is first woman elected to Congress.

April 2, 1917: In Rankin's first vote in Congress, she votes against the U.S. entering World War I.

1919 – 1940: Rankin is a private citizen, working for organizations, speaking out and lobbying for peace and women's and children's rights.

1940: After World War II erupts in Europe, Rankin decides the best way to argue for peace is to return to Congress.

November 5, 1940: At age 60, Rankin, running on a peace platform, is elected to her second term as a congresswoman from Montana.

December 7, 1941: Japan attacks the U.S. Navy at Pearl Harbor, Hawaii.

December 8, 1941: The next day, President Franklin Roosevelt asks Congress to declare war on Japan. Rankin is the only member of Congress to vote no.

1943: At age 62, Rankin leaves Congress with little accomplished.

1943 – 1965: Rankin is mostly out of the public eye, living in Georgia and sometimes in Montana and traveling the world extensively, including seven trips to India. She is a strong follower of India's leader Mahatma Gandhi and his pacifist philosophy.

1966: The United States is fighting in the Vietnam War. Thousands of U.S. soldiers are dying. The anti-war movement is growing in the U.S. Rankin, who turns 86, begins to speak out against the war.

May 1967: Rankin speaks to anti-war activists in Atlanta, Georgia.

January 15, 1968: Rankin leads thousands of women in an anti-war march in Washington, D.C., as part of the Jeannette Rankin Brigade.

October 15, 1969: Jeannette Rankin joins the national Moratorium Day protest, speaking out against the Vietnam War at the University of Georgia.

June 11, 1970: Rankin celebrates her 90th birthday with a dinner in her honor given by members of Congress in Washington, D.C.

February 12, 1972: Rankin is called the "world's outstanding living feminist" by the National Organization of Women, at an event in which she is honored and inducted into the Susan B. Anthony Hall of Fame.

May 18, 1973: Rankin dies in Carmel, California, a few weeks short of her 93rd birthday.

<u>CONGRESSWOMAN JEANNETTE RANKIN'S STATEMENT REGARDING
HER "NO" VOTE ON DECEMBER 8, 1941:</u>

*On December 8, 1941--immediately following her "no" vote on a declaration
of war against Japan--Montana Congresswoman Jeannette Rankin retired to
her office and composed an explanation of her vote. Her staff
distributed this statement to newspapers throughout her Montana district.*

****

Today I voted against the resolution declaring war on the Japanese
empire. Inasmuch as my vote was the only one cast against our entry, I
feel I owe the people of my district a statement.

As those of you who listened in over the radio are aware, I tried
repeatedly to get the floor to ask some questions. I felt there were not
enough facts before us--especially since most of them were based on
brief, unconfirmed reports--to justify such hasty action. The address of
the President did not give us any additional facts.

After a speech of little more than 500 words and a debate which
lasted only 18 minutes, the roll was called in the House, and the die was
cast which hurled our country into the conflict.

Before we entered the last World War, four days were consumed in
debating all phases of the issue before the vote was taken. Every
argument used today was the same as in the last war, except this time the
speed was so great that it prevented any answer or questions. Had the
vote to go to war been unanimous, it would have been a totalitarian vote,
one not in keeping with our American way of life.

When I cast the only vote against war, I remembered the promises I
had made during my campaign for election to do everything possible to
keep this country out of war. I was thinking of the pledges I had made
to the mothers and fathers of Montana that I would do all in my power to
prevent their sons being slaughtered on foreign battlefields.

While I believed, with the other members of the House, that the
stories which had come over the radio were probably true, still I
believed that such a momentous vote--one which would mean peace or war
for our country--should be based on more authentic evidence than the
radio reports now at hand.

Sending our boys to the Orient will not protect this country. We
are all for every measure which will mean defense for our land, but
taking our army and navy across thousands of miles of ocean to fight and
die certainly cannot come under the heading of protecting our shores.

But now we are sending American men and boys into a war to
'protect' the United States, and doing it based only on a few brief,
incomplete radio reports which do not pretend to give the entire story.

It may be that it is right for us to enter the conflict with Japan.
If so, it is my belief that all the facts surrounding the present
situation should be brought into the open and given to the Congress and
the American people.

So in casting my vote today, I voted my convictions and redeemed my
campaign pledges. I feel I voted as the mothers would have had me vote.

****

388-1

*Congresswoman Jeannette Rankin's statement on December 8, 1941, after casting the
only vote against the U.S. entering World War II. (Jeannette Rankin Peace Center)*

Selected Bibliography

Burnette, Lindsey. *Jeannette Rankin Brigade*. University of North Carolina, at Chapel Hill, Department of American Studies, April 19, 2018.

Boundary Stones, WETA's Washington, D.C. History Blog, *The Jeannette Rankin Brigade*, https://blogs.weta.org/boundarystones/2016/08/24/jeannette-rankin-brigade, August 24, 2016.

Britannica.com, https://www.britannica.com/event/United-States-presidential-election-of-1916.

Brozan, Nadine. "Crusading Forerunner of Women's Lib." *The New York Times*, January 24, 1972.

ConstitutionalCenter.org, various documents.

Dunlap, David W. "1916: Abhors War, Wins Elections, Whips Up Lemon Meringue." *The New York Times*, July 28, 2016.

Giles, Kevin S. *One Woman Against War: The Jeannette Rankin Story*. St. Petersburg, Florida: BookLocker.com, 2016.

The History Channel website at www.history.com/topics/world-war-i/lusitania. *September 1, 1939: Germans Invade Poland* and other articles.

The History Learning website at www.historylearningsite.co.uk/world-war-one/timeline-of-world-war-one/.

Hunter, Marjorie. "Remembering Again." *The New York Times*, April 27, 1985.

Josephson, Hannah. *Jeannette Rankin: First Lady in Congress.* Indianapolis, IN, and New York: The Bobbs-Merrill Company, Inc., 1974.

Kidney, Gary. "One Vote Against War." Warfare History Network website, https://warfarehistorynetwork.com/daily/wwii/one-vote-against-war/, November 21, 2016.

Kluckhohn, Frank L. "U.S Declares War, Unity in Congress, Only One Negative Vote…" *The New York Times*, December 9, 1941.

Lincoln Journal Star, "Jeannette Rankin Dies," May 20, 1973.

Lopach, James and Luckowski, Jean. *A Chronology and Primary Sources for Teaching about Jeannette Rankin*, University of Montana, undated.

Marx, Trish. *Jeannette Rankin: First Lady of Congress*. New York: Simon & Schuster, 2006.

Matthews, Lafayette. *The Jeannette Rankin Brigade*. https://blogs.weta.org/boundarystones/201608/24/Jeannette-rankin-brigade, August 24, 2016.

McFadden, Robert. "Ex-Rep. Jeannette Rankin Dies; First Woman in Congress, 92." *The New York Times*, May 20, 1973.

Military Factory website, www.militaryfactory.com/vietnam/casualties.asp, for various articles.

Montana Historical Society Research Center, Helena, MT, various photographs.

National Archives, *Vietnam War U.S. Military Fatal Casualty Statistics*, http://www.archives.gov/research/military/vietnam-war/casualty-statistics.

The National World War II Museum website www.Nationalww2museum.org. *Remembering Pearl Harbor: A Pearl Harbor Fact Sheet*.

The New York Times. "The House Beautiful." October 13, 1916.

The New York Times. "Jeannette Rankin Here: Woman Representative from Montana to Represent All Parties." February 25, 1917.

O'Brien, Mary Barmeyer. *Jeannette Rankin: Bright Star in the Big Sky*. Rowman & Littlefield, 2016.

President Woodrow Wilson's speech to Congress, delivered April 2, 1917, asking for a declaration of war for World War I, https://wwi.lib.edu/index.php/Wilson's_War_Message_to_Congress.

President Franklin D. Roosevelt's speech to Congress, delivered December 8, 1941, asking for a declaration of war for World War II (against Japan), https://www.archives.gov/publications/prologue/2001/winter/crafting-day-of-infamy-speech.html and http://www.fdrlibrary.marist.edu/_resources/images/msf/msfb0002.

Rankin, Jeannette, *Congressional Record*, December 8, 1942.

The Raucous Rooster website http://theraucousrooster.com/2018/01/15/january-15-1968-sisterhood-powerful-jeannette-rankin-brigade-marches-capitol/, *January 15, 1968: Sisterhood is Powerful – The Jeannette Rankin Brigade Marches on the Capitol*, January 15, 2018.

Smith, Norma. *Jeannette Rankin: America's Conscience.* Helena, Montana: Montana Historical Society Press, 2002.

Swarthmore College Peace Collection, Swarthmore College, Swarthmore, PA, various photographs.

U.S. National Archives and Records Administration, various documents.

Wachtell, Cynthia. "A Hundred Years of Misogyny: Hillary Clinton, Jeannette Rankin, and the 'First Woman' Elections of 1916 and 2016." *Huffington Post,* October 25, 2016.

Woelfle, Gretchen. *Jeannette Rankin: Political Pioneer.* Honesdale, PA: Calkins Creek, 20007.

Other various historical websites

Sources for Quotations

Page 8: "She was going to be out there fighting…" (Giles, Kevin S. *One Woman Against War: The Jeannette Rankin Story*. St. Petersburg, Florida. BookLocker.com, 2016, p. 15)

P. 18: "I took the dearest… sweetest little boy…" (Smith, Norma. *Jeannette Rankin: America's Conscience*. Helena, Montana: Montana Historical Society Press, 2002, p. 51, and Giles, p. 45)

P. 20: "I will never forget it…" (Smith, p. 55)

P. 22: "An audience of 300 people stood…" (Smith, p. 62)

P. 24: "It's beautiful and right that a woman should nurse her sick children…" (Smith, p. 63)

P. 26: "Women need votes to end sweatshops." (Smith, p. 65)

P. 26: "…one of the best schooled and enthusiastic suffragettes to be found in America." (Smith, p. 69)

P. 28: "Ask your fathers why they won't let your mothers vote." (Smith, p. 82)

P. 28: "When Miss Rankin came forward to speak…" (Smith, p. 87)

P. 33: "The primal motive for my seeking a seat in the national Congress…" (Giles, p. 54)

P. 34: "There are hundreds of men…" (Woelfle, Gretchen. *Jeannette Rankin: Political Pioneer.* Honesdale, PA: Calkins Creek, 20007, p. 43)

P. 36: "Why – Jeannette Rankin – you have given Suffrage…" (Giles p. 108)

P. 36: "Maid of Missoula." (Giles, p. 110)

P. 36: "I'm not nervous about going to Congress…" (Woelfle, p. 46)

P. 42: "The world must be made safe for democracy." (President Woodrow Wilson's address to Congress on April 2, 1917, https://wwi.lib.edu/index.php/Wilson's_War_Message_to_Con gress.)

P. 43: "Vote a man's vote." (Josephson, Hannah. *Jeannette Rankin: First Lady in Congress.* Indianapolis, IN, and New York: The Bobbs-Merrill Company, Inc., 1974, p. 73)

P. 43: "I want to stand by my country…" (Josephson, p. 76)

P. 44: "… a member of the [German] army in the United States." (Josephson, p. 77)

P. 44: "Our Congress Lady is sure enough a joker…" (Smith, p. 113)

P. 45: "Montana's Congresswoman is Now Very Popular…" (Smith p. 113)

P. 45: "Never for one second…" (Josephson, p. 74)

P. 48: "We as a nation were born in a land…" (Smith, p. 124 and Giles, p. 195)

P. 51: "The work of educating the world for peace…" (Smith, p. 158, and Giles, p. 224)

P. 53: "… for toilet paper…" (Woelfle, p. 62)

P. 53: "… cherished her trees…" (Woelfle, p. 63)

P. 55: "No woman can with honor…" (Josephson, p. 120)

P. 55: "She made all preparations for war…" (Giles, p. 236)

P. 55: "Up pops the devil." (Giles, p. 249)

P. 57: "You can no more win a war than you can an earthquake." (Josephson, p. 135)

P. 60: "Talk to your parents…" (Josephson, p. 155)

P. 60: "Someday, one of you may…" (Josephson, p. 155)

P. 61: "By voting for me…" (Smith, p. 176)

P. 62: "I am still trying to keep our men…" (Giles, p. 300)

P. 65: "I got into my car and left the office…" (Woelfle, p. 74)

P. 66: "Yesterday, December 7, 1941, a date which will live in infamy…" and "I believe that I interpret the will…" (President Franklin D. Roosevelt's address to Congress on December 8, 1941, http://docs.fdrlibrary.marist.edu/tmirhdee.html)

P. 67: "Mr. Speaker, I object…" and "You're out of order." (Josephson, p. 161)

P. 67: "Mr. Speaker! …" (Josephson, p. 161)

P. 67: "Miss Rankin is on her feet… (Giles, p. 315)

P. 67: "As a woman…" (Josephson, p. 162 and Giles, p. 316)

P. 68: "Montana is 110 percent against you." (Giles, p. 321)

P. 68: "When I cast the only vote…" (Congresswoman Rankin's statement on December 8, 1941, after voting against the U.S. entering World War II, courtesy of Jeannette Rankin Peace Center)

P. 69: "You made an ass out of yourself..."; "I hope a Jap bomb drops..."; "... petty-coated idiot."; and "Resign, you poor sissy." (Giles, p. 321-322)

P. 69: "Either Miss Rankin is stupid..." (Woelfle, p. 76)

P. 70: "She dismissed the bombing as lightly..." (Giles, p. 323)

P. 70: "In all of history no man..." (Giles, p. 329)

P. 70: "Well – look at Jeannette Rankin..." (Josephson, p. 162 and Woelfle, p. 76-77)

P. 70: "Jeannette was completely out of step..." (Smith, p. 168)

P. 71: "... why did the President..." (*Congressional Record*, December 8, 1942)

P. 73: "... used spiritual power ..." (Smith, p. 201)

P. 76: "I have not come to Iran to talk..." (Smith, p. 204)

P. 76: "Why talk about it? ..." (Smith, p. 204)

P. 81: "It isn't a question of war against Germany..." (Smith, p. 209)

P. 82: "It is unconscionable that 10,000 boys..." (Josephson, p. 182)

P. 84: "We waste our money…" (Giles, p. 384)

P. 85: "… ninety years young…" (Giles, p. 389)

P. 86: "… saver with a great heart…" (Giles, p. 390)

P. 86: "We must have absolutely unilateral disarmament." (Giles, p. 394)

P. 88: "The world's outstanding living feminist." (Giles, p. 394)

P. 88: "Women must devote all…" (Giles, p. 394)

P. 92: "I believe then as I do now…" (Giles, p. 418)

Photograph Credits

Book cover, Rankin photo on left. (Montana Historical Society Research Center)

Book cover, Rankin photo on right. (Montana Historical Society Research Center)

Rankin photo after dedication page. (National Photo Company Collection, Library of Congress, via Wikimedia Commons)

P. 1: Jeannette Rankin in her 80s. (Jeannette Rankin Exhibit at Georgia World Congress Center, via AVOC)

P. 2: Jeannette Rankin leading the Jeannette Rankin Brigade in a protest march against the Vietnam War in Washington, D.C., January 15, 1968. (Bettmann, Getty Images)

P. 4: A ranch in Montana, circa 1880. (William Henry Jackson, U.S. National Archives, via Wikimedia Commons)

P. 5: The site of the Battle of Little Bighorn in Montana, fought in 1876. (Wikimedia Commons)

P. 6: John Rankin. (Montana Historical Society Research Center)

P. 8: Rankin family photo, circa 1890. (Montana Historical Society Research Center)

P. 9: Jeannette Rankin, lower left, with friends or classmates, circa early 1890s. (Montana Historical Society Research Center)

P. 10: American Indian land near Missoula, Montana. (Archives and Special Collections, Mansfield Library, University of Montana)

P. 11: The old Montana State University campus in Missoula, circa 1900. (University of Montana Historical Archives, via Wikimedia Commons)

P. 12: Jeannette Rankin studying in the lab at college. (Montana Historical Society Research Center)

P. 13: Rankin family photo. (Montana Historical Society Research Center)

P. 15: Lower East Side of New York City, circa 1900. (Detroit Publishing Company, Library of Congress, via Wikimedia Commons)

P. 16: San Francisco in ruins after the earthquake and fire of 1906. (The H.C. White Company, via Wikimedia Commons)

P. 17: Booker T. Washington. (Wikimedia Commons)

P. 18: New York City's Lower East Side, circa 1900. (Wikimedia Commons)

P. 19: Jeannette Rankin with relative or friend. (Montana Historical Society Research Center)

P. 21: Suffrage workers in the state of Washington hanging posters to promote women gaining the right to vote, circa 1910. (University of Washington Libraries, Special Collections, Asahel Curtis, photographer, A. Curtis 19943)

P. 23: Women voting in Seattle, WA, in 1911. (McClure's, Seattle Public Library, via Wikimedia Commons)

P. 24: Jeannette Rankin holding a suffrage flag during the campaign to get women the right to vote in Montana. (Montana Historical Society Research Center)

P. 25: Protest marchers after the Triangle Shirtwaist Fire in New York City in 1911. (U.S. National Archives, via Wikimedia Commons)

P. 26: A suffrage rally on Pennsylvania Avenue in Washington, D.C., on March 3, 1913. (Photo by George Grantham Bain, Library of Congress, via Wikimedia Commons)

P. 27: A suffrage car procession nearing Washington, D.C., on July 31, 1913. (Photo by W.R. Ross, Library of Congress, via Wikimedia Commons)

P. 28: Women working for suffrage in Montana, circa 1914. (Montana Historical Society Research Center)

P. 29: The suffrage ballot in Montana for November 3, 1914. (*The Suffrage Daily News*, via Montanawomenshistory.org)

P. 31: Jeannette Rankin in a 1916 campaign photo. (Montana Historical Society Research Center)

P. 32: Jeannette Rankin and her brother, Wellington, around the time she ran for Congress. (Montana Historical Society Research Center)

P. 33: Jeannette Rankin campaigning in Montana. (Montana Historical Society Research Center)

P. 35: Jeannette Rankin's signed photograph. (Library of Congress, via Wikimedia Commons)

P. 37: Congresswoman Rankin after being elected to Congress. (Montana Historical Society Research Center)

P. 38: Painting showing the sinking of the Lusitania by a German submarine, on May 7, 1915. (German Federal Archives, via Wikimedia Commons)

P. 39: Congresswoman Rankin speaking to supporters, just before going to the Capitol on her first official day as a congresswoman in Washington, on April 2, 1917. (Photo by C.T. Chapman, Library of Congress, via Wikimedia Commons)

P. 40: Congresswoman Rankin about to be driven to the Capitol on her first day in Congress. (National Photo Company Collection, Library of Congress, via Wikimedia Commons)

P. 41: President Woodrow Wilson asking Congress to declare war on Germany, April 2, 1917. (Library of Congress, via Wikimedia Commons)

P. 42: German soldiers fighting in World War I. (Photo by the German Army, via Wikimedia Commons)

P. 44: Headline after Congress voted to enter World War I. (*The Daily Missoulian*, courtesy Jeannette Rankin Peace Center)

P. 45: Rep. Jeannette Rankin with some of the Congressmen who voted against war in April 1917. (National Council for Prevention of War Records, Photograph Collection, Swarthmore College Peace Collection)

P. 47: Congresswoman Jeannette Rankin, on right, during a suffrage event in Washington, circa 1917. (Library of Congress, via Wikimedia Commons)

P. 48: Congresswoman Jeannette Rankin speaking before Congress in 1917. (Wikimedia Commons)

P. 50: Women voting after the 19th Amendment was passed. (Library of Congress, vis Bustle.com)

P. 52: Destruction in a Belgian forest from World War I. (Australian War Memorial, via Wikimedia Commons)

P. 53: Jeannette Rankin outside her home in Georgia in the 1920s. (Montana Historical Society Research Center)

P. 54: Men line up outside a soup kitchen in Chicago during the Depression. (U.S. National Archives, via Wikimedia Commons)

P. 56: Jeannette Rankin meeting with Senator Gerald Nye in Washington in 1935. (Montana Historical Society Research Center)

P. 57: Italian soldiers fighting in Ethiopia in 1935. (Library of Congress, via Wikimedia Commons)

P. 58: German troops march through Warsaw, Poland, after they invaded the country in 1939. (U.S. National Archives, via Wikimedia Commons)

P. 59: Jeannette Rankin's campaign photograph from 1940. (Montana Historical Society Research Center)

P. 61: Firefighters putting out a fire in London after a German bombing. (U.S. National Archives, via Wikimedia Commons)

P. 63: The Japanese attack at Pearl Harbor on December 7, 1941. (U.S. National Archives, via Wikimedia Commons)

P. 64: Newspaper headline announcing Japanese attack. (*The Boston Daily Globe*)

P. 66: President Franklin Roosevelt delivering his address to Congress on December 8, 1941. (U.S. National Archives, via Wikimedia Commons)

P. 68: Congresswoman Rankin in a phone booth calling Capitol Police for assistance, after being harassed for voting against war. (Bettmann, Getty Images)

P. 69: Newspaper headline announcing U.S. declaration of war against Japan. (*The Washington Daily News*, courtesy of Jeannette Rankin Peace Center)

P. 71: Congresswoman Rankin's statement in the Congressional Record on Dec. 8, 1942. (*Congressional Record*, Dec. 8, 1942, via Jeannette Rankin Peace Center)

P. 72: Stalingrad, Russia, after a long battle in 1943. (RIA Novosti Archive, via Wikimedia Commons)

P. 73: Mahatma Gandhi, India's leader. (Wikimedia Commons)

P. 74: Jeannette Rankin traveling in India. (Montana Historical Society Research Center)

P. 75: Jeannette Rankin at the Pyramids in Egypt. (Montana Historical Society Research Center)

P. 77: Jeannette Rankin, circa late 1960s. (Montana Historical Society Research Center)

P. 78: Dr. Martin Luther King Jr. on the steps of the Lincoln Memorial on August 28, 1963, the day he delivered his "I have a dream" speech. (Wikimedia Commons)

P. 79: Two soldiers await a helicopter to evacuate them and their comrade, who was killed in battle in Vietnam, 1966. (Photo by Pfc. L. Paul Epley, U.S. National Archives, via Wikimedia Commons)

P. 80: Vietnam War protestors in Washington, D.C., in 1967. (Photo by Frank Wolfe, via Wikimedia Commons)

P. 81: Jeannette Rankin at a press conference with Coretta Scott King, Dr. Martin Luther King Jr.'s wife, speaking out against the Vietnam War. (Bettmann, Getty Images)

P. 82: Jeannette Rankin, center with glasses, with Jeannette Rankin Brigade during 1968 march to the Capitol to protest U.S. fighting in the Vietnam War. (Getty Images)

P. 83: Jeannette Rankin Brigade button. (Mildred Scott Olmsted Papers: Button, Pin and Ribbon Collection, Swarthmore College Peace Collection)

P. 84: Jeannette Rankin meeting with Senator Mike Mansfield after the protest march to the Capitol by the Jeannette Rankin Brigade, Jan. 15, 1968. (Montana Historical Society Research Center)

P. 85: Anti-war protests by students at Florida State University, Tallahassee, Florida, in 1970. (State Archives of Florida, Florida Memory, via Wikimedia Commons)

P. 86: Congresswoman Rankin leaving the White House in 1917. (Photo by Harris & Ewing, Library of Congress, via Wikimedia Commons)

P. 87: Rankin receiving a prestigious award from the National Organization of Women on February 12, 1972. (FPG, Hulton Archive, Getty Images)

P. 89: Jeannette Rankin, circa early 1970s. (U.S. Congress, via Wikimedia Commons)

P. 90: Hillary Clinton speaking in 2016. (Photo by Lorie Shaull, via Wikimedia Commons)

P. 91: In 1939, Jeannette Rankin testified before a Congressional Committee. (Photo by Harris & Ewing, Library of Congress, via Wikimedia Commons)

P. 93: The statue of Jeannette Rankin in the National Statutory Hall in the Capitol, in Washington, D.C. (U.S. Capitol, via Wikimedia Commons)

Author's Acknowledgements

In my research, I relied extensively on the many fine biographies and articles written about Jeannette Rankin over the years. In particular, I relied on the following biographies in my research: *One Woman Against War: The Jeannette Rankin Story,* by Kevin S. Giles; *Jeannette Rankin: First Lady in Congress,* by Hannah Josephson; *Jeannette Rankin: First Lady of Congress,* by Trish Marx; *Jeannette Rankin: America's Conscience,* by Norma Smith; and *Jeannette Rankin: Political Pioneer,* by Gretchen Woelfle.

I wish to thank the following individuals for reviewing my manuscript and making suggestions: Kevin S. Giles, author of the previously mentioned *One Woman Against War: The Jeannette Rankin Story,* the best single biography I read on Rankin; and Betsy Mulligan-Dague, executive director, Jeannette Rankin Peace Center, Missoula, MT. And, as always, I wish to thank my wife, Emily Russo, for reading multiple drafts and always making helpful comments.

Thanks to the Montana Historical Society Research Center and its patient and helpful staff, including Laura Tretter, technical services librarian, and Kellyn Younggren, photograph archivist, in helping me find appropriate photographs for my book and then granting me permission to use the photos in the book.

Also, thank you to Swarthmore College's Peace Center, particularly Wendy E. Chmielewski, PhD., George R. Cooley Curator, and Mary Beth Sigado, for helping me find and granting me access to photographs in their collection for my book.

Also, thanks to Getty Images, the University of Washington library, and the Mansfield Library, University of Montana, Missoula, for providing me with photos for the book.

Thanks to Jessica Jewell, administrative assistant to Executive Director Betsy Mulligan-Dague, Jeannette Rankin Peace Center, for assisting with research.

A special thanks to my collaborators, Ashley Byland of Redbird Designs, for her beautiful cover design, and to Jason Anderson of Polgarus Studio, for his wonderful layout and incredible patience as I worked through the many changes in my manuscript.

And, as always, a very special thanks to Emily and my two daughters, Mabel and Maisy, for their patience and understanding as I continue to pursue my passion of writing children's books. Without them giving me encouragement and the time to work, I could not succeed. I am lucky to have such a loving family. I love my three girls (and Hazel, our dog) all very much.

Author's Biography

Credit: Rashidah De Vore

Peter Aronson is a former journalist, a former attorney and now a children's book author. He lives in New York City with his wife, Emily, and two teenage daughters, Mabel and Maisy, and their dog, Hazel.

Peter has a strong desire to tell stories about important and inspiring individuals who are not well known. He started his Groundbreaker Series (biographies about extraordinary people doing extraordinary things) for middle-grade readers for that purpose.

This book is the second in the series. The first book in the series, published in July 2018, was _Bronislaw Huberman: From Child Prodigy to Hero, the Violinist who Saved Jewish Musicians from the Holocaust_.

Peter also is working on a trilogy of novels for middle-grade readers. Mandalay Hawk and her friends, three precocious 14-year olds, tackle the world's biggest problems. _Mandalay Hawk's Dilemma: The United States of Anthropocene_, the first book in the trilogy, follows a kid's movement unlike any other. KRAAP – Kids Revolt Against Adult Power. How else are you going to stop global warming? The book is due out in 2019.

Info about Peter's books can be found at
www.peteraronsonbooks.com.
Peter can be emailed at peter@peteraronsonbooks.com.

Thank you.